Is anything too hard
for the Lord?

GENESIS 18:14 NKJV

20 THINGS GOD CAN'T DO

Dr. Criswell Freeman

Copyright © 2013 by Freeman–Smith, a division of Worthy Media, Inc.

ISBN 978-1-60587-533-0

Published by Freeman-Smith, a division of Worthy Media, Inc.,
134 Franklin Road, Suite 200, Brentwood, Tennessee 37027.

The quoted ideas expressed in this book (but not Scripture verses) are not, in all cases, exact quotations, as some have been edited for clarity and brevity. In all cases, the author has attempted to maintain the speaker's original intent. In some cases, quoted material for this book was obtained from secondary sources, primarily print media. While every effort was made to ensure the accuracy of these sources, the accuracy cannot be guaranteed. For additions, deletions, corrections, or clarifications in future editions of this text, please write Freeman-Smith.

Cover Design by Scott Williams/ Richmond & Williams
Page Layout by Bart Dawson

Printed in the United States of America

1 2 3 4 5—SBI—17 16 15 14 13

20
THINGS
GOD
CAN'T DO

Dr. Criswell Freeman

FREEMAN-SMITH

TABLE OF CONTENTS

God also bound himself with an oath,
so that those who received the promise could be
perfectly sure that he would never change his mind.
So God has given us both his promise and his oath.
These two things are unchangeable because
it is impossible for God to lie. Therefore,
we who have fled to him for refuge can take
new courage, for we can hold on
to his promise with confidence.

—

HEBREWS 6:17-18 NLT

INTRODUCTION

Because He is all-powerful, God can do all things. However, God most certainly does not do all things. There are some things that He will not do—indeed cannot do—because He has promised not to do them.

God has given us a book of promises upon which we can all depend. That book, of course, is the Holy Bible. This text details 20 things that God, through His inspired Word, has promised never to do. And, because the Lord always keeps His word, we can experience peace and confidence, knowing that He will never betray us.

God has promised that He will never abandon us. He has promised that He cannot deceive us. He has promised that He will never withhold His forgiveness when we forgive others. And, He has promised that He cannot separate us from the love of His only begotten Son. These pledges are unalterable; they will endure throughout eternity. When you stake your future, and your life, upon these pledges, you won't be disappointed.

So, for the next 20 days, please try this experiment. Read a chapter each day, and think about the things that God cannot do. But don't stop there. While you're considering the things that God has promised not to do, also praise Him for the things He has already done, and for the things He most certainly will do for you, for your loved ones, and for mankind.

1

GOD CANNOT BREAK A PROMISE

No, I will not break my covenant;
I will not take back a single word I said.

—

PSALM 89:34 NLT

THE BIG IDEA

God has made many promises to you,
and He will keep every single one of them.
Your job is to trust God's Word and to live
accordingly.

YOU CAN TRUST GOD'S WORD
BECAUSE HE NEVER BREAKS A PROMISE

God has made quite a few promises to you, and He will keep every single one of them. Elisabeth Elliot observed, "We have ample evidence that the Lord is able to guide. The promises cover every imaginable situation. All we need to do is to take the hand he stretches out." And her words apply to you and to every situation you will ever encounter.

Have you endured a painful loss? The Bible promises that God can ease your pain. Are you fearful, exhausted, fretful, or troubled? God promises that He will strengthen and protect you, now and throughout eternity. Has your world been turned upside down by unexpected events that were beyond your control? God promises that He is sufficient to meet your every need.

Whatever challenges you may face, whatever troubles you encounter, God is with you, and He stands ready to protect you.

Vance Havner observed, "It takes calm, thoughtful, prayerful meditation on the Word to extract its deepest nourishment." How true. God's Word can be a roadmap to a place of righteousness and abundance. Make it your roadmap. God's wisdom can be a light to guide your steps. Claim it as your light today, tomorrow, and every day of your life as you walk confidently in the footsteps of God's only begotten Son. And while you're walking with God's Son, please remember that the Lord will not—indeed cannot—break a promise. He is always faithful, and you can always depend on Him.

A mighty fortress is our God,
a bulwark never failing;
Our helper He, amid the flood
of mortal ills prevailing;
For still our ancient foe doth seek
to work us woe;
His craft and power are great,
armed with cruel hate,
Our earth is not his equal.

—

MARTIN LUTHER

MORE FROM GOD'S WORD

As for God, His way is perfect; the word of the Lord is proven; He is a shield to all who trust in Him.

PSALM 18:30 NKJV

Whatever God has promised gets stamped with the Yes of Jesus. In him, this is what we preach and pray, the great Amen, God's Yes and our Yes together, gloriously evident.

2 CORINTHIANS 1:20 MSG

What time I am afraid, I will trust in thee.

PSALM 56:3 KJV

Trust in the Lord with all your heart, and do not rely on your own understanding; think about Him in all your ways, and He will guide you on the right paths.

PROVERBS 3:5-6 HCSB

Let us hold on to the confession of our hope without wavering, for He who promised is faithful.

HEBREWS 10:23 HCSB

MORE BIG IDEAS ABOUT GOD'S PROMISES

Never doubt in the dark what God told you in the light.

V. RAYMOND EDMAN

The meaning of hope isn't just some flimsy wishing. It's a firm confidence in God's promises—that he will ultimately set things right.

SHEILA WALSH

We can have full confidence in God's promises because we can have full faith in His character.

FRANKLIN GRAHAM

Faith is confidence in the promises of God or confidence that God will do what He has promised.

CHARLES STANLEY

In Biblical worship you do not find the repetition of a phrase; instead, you find the worshipers rehearsing the character of God and His ways, reminding Him of His faithfulness and His wonderful promises.

KAY ARTHUR

Gather the riches of God's promises which can strengthen you in the time when there will be no freedom.

CORRIE TEN BOOM

We honor God by asking for great things when they are a part of His promise. We dishonor Him and cheat ourselves when we ask for molehills where He has promised mountains.

VANCE HAVNER

God's promises are medicine for the broken heart. Let Him comfort you. And, after He has comforted you, try to share that comfort with somebody else. It will do both of you good.

WARREN WIERSBE

It is faith that what happens to me matters to God as well as to me that gives me joy, that promises me that I am eternally the subject of God's compassion, and that assures me that the compassion was manifested most brilliantly when God came to us in a stable in Bethlehem.

MADELEINE L'ENGLE

Fear and doubt are conquered
by a faith that rejoices.
And faith can rejoice because
the promises of God are
as certain as God Himself.

—

KAY ARTHUR

THOUGHTS ABOUT WHAT GOD CAN DO

_____

_____

_____

_____

_____

_____

_____

_____

_____

A PRAYER FOR TODAY

Lord, Your Holy Word contains promises, and I will trust them. I will use the Bible as my guide, and I will trust You, Lord, to speak to me through Your Holy Spirit and through Your Holy Word, this day and forever. Amen

2

GOD CANNOT SEPARATE YOU FROM CHRIST'S LOVE

For I am persuaded that neither death nor life,
nor angels nor rulers, nor things present,
nor things to come, nor powers, nor height,
nor depth, nor any other created thing will have
the power to separate us from the love of God
that is in Christ Jesus our Lord!

ROMANS 8:38-39 HCSB

THE BIG IDEA

Jesus loves you. His love can
—and should—be the cornerstone
and the touchstone of your life.

HIS AMAZING LOVE

God's love for you is bigger and better than you can imagine. In fact, God's love is far too big to comprehend (in this lifetime). But of this you can be sure: God loves you so much that He sent His Son Jesus to come to this earth and to die for you. And, when you accepted Jesus into your heart, God gave you a gift that is more precious than gold: the gift of eternal life. It's a gift that He will never take away.

The words of Romans 8 make this promise: that absolutely nothing "will have the power to separate us from the love of God that is in Christ Jesus." What a glorious promise!

God gave you a gift that is more precious than gold.

Sometimes, in the crush of your daily duties, God may seem far away, but He is not. God is everywhere you have ever been and everywhere you will ever go. He is with you night and day; He knows your thoughts and He hears your prayers. When you earnestly seek Him, you will find Him because He is here, waiting patiently for you to reach out to Him. So take time today to thank Him for a love that is too big to understand with your head, but not too big to feel with your heart.

MORE FROM GOD'S WORD

For the Lord is good, and His love is eternal; His faithfulness endures through all generations.

PSALM 100:5 HCSB

For God loved the world in this way: He gave His only Son, so that everyone who believes in Him will not perish but have eternal life.

JOHN 3:16 HCSB

[Because of] the Lord's faithful love we do not perish, for His mercies never end. They are new every morning; great is Your faithfulness!

LAMENTATIONS 3:22-23 HCSB

Help me, Lord my God; save me according to Your faithful love.

PSALM 109:26 HCSB

Whoever is wise will observe these things, and they will understand the lovingkindness of the Lord.

PSALM 107:43 NKJV

MORE BIG IDEAS ABOUT CHRIST'S LOVE

The richest meaning of your life is contained in the idea that Christ loved you enough to give His life for you.

CALVIN MILLER

Jesus has been consistently affectionate and true to us. He has shared his great wealth with us. How can we doubt the all-powerful, all-sufficient Lord?

C. H. SPURGEON

Christ is like a river that is continually flowing. There are always fresh supplies of water coming from the fountainhead, so that a man may live by it and be supplied with water all his life. So Christ is an ever-flowing fountain; he is continually supplying his people, and the fountain is not spent. They who live upon Christ may have fresh supplies from him for all eternity; they may have an increase of blessedness that is new, and new still, and which never will come to an end.

JONATHAN EDWARDS

Jesus: the proof of God's love.

PHILIP YANCEY

So Jesus came, stripping himself of everything as he came—omnipotence, omniscience, omnipresence—everything except love. "He emptied himself" (Philippians 2:7), emptied himself of everything except love. Love—his only protection, his only weapon, his only method.

E. STANLEY JONES

If you come to Christ, you will always have the option of an ever-present friend. You don't have to dial long-distance. He'll be with you every step of the way.

BILL HYBELS

No man ever loved like Jesus. He taught the blind to see and the dumb to speak. He died on the cross to save us. He bore our sins. And now God says, "Because He did, I can forgive you."

BILLY GRAHAM

Jesus means Savior, revealing His God-ordained mission to present Himself as the Lamb, without spot or blemish, Who would make atonement for the sin of the world through the sacrifice of Himself on the altar of the cross.

ANNE GRAHAM LOTZ

Behold, behold the wondrous love,
That ever flows from God above
Through Christ His only Son,
Who gave His precious blood
our souls to save.

—

FANNY CROSBY

THOUGHTS ABOUT WHAT GOD CAN DO

_____

_____

_____

_____

_____

_____

_____

_____

A PRAYER FOR TODAY

Thank You, Lord, for Your Son. His love is boundless, infinite, and eternal. Today, let me pause and reflect upon Christ's love for me, and let me share that love with all those who cross my path. And, as an expression of my love for Him, let me share Christ's saving message with a world that desperately needs His grace. Amen

3

GOD CANNOT
IGNORE OR
ABANDON YOU

For the eyes of the Lord range throughout the earth to strengthen those whose hearts are fully committed to him.

—

2 CHRONICLES 16:9 NIV

THE BIG IDEA

God knows everything about
His creation and about you.
The Lord is watching over you today,
tomorrow, and forever.

GOD IS NEVER DISTANT

God is everywhere we have ever been and everywhere we will ever be. When we turn to Him often, we are blessed by His presence. But, if we ignore God's presence or rebel against it altogether, the world in which we live soon becomes a spiritual wasteland.

Since God is everywhere, we are free to sense His presence whenever we take the time to quiet our souls and turn our prayers to Him. But sometimes, amid the incessant demands of everyday life, we turn our thoughts far from God; when we do, we suffer.

Do you set aside quiet moments each day to offer praise to God? You should. During these moments of stillness, you can sense the infinite love and power of our Lord. The familiar words of Psalm 46:10 remind us to "Be still, and know that I am God" (KJV). When we do so, we encounter the awesome presence of our loving Heavenly Father.

Are you tired, discouraged, or fearful? Be comforted because God is with you. Are you bitter? Talk with God and seek His guidance. Are you celebrating a great victory? Thank God and praise Him. He is the Giver of all things good. In whatever condition you find yourself—whether you are happy or sad, victorious or vanquished, troubled or triumphant—celebrate God's presence. And be comforted in the knowledge that God is not just near. He is here.

MORE FROM GOD'S WORD

No, I will not abandon you as orphans—I will come to you.

JOHN 14:18 NLT

The Lord is near all who call out to Him, all who call out to Him with integrity. He fulfills the desires of those who fear Him; He hears their cry for help and saves them.

PSALM 145:18-19 HCSB

Surely goodness and mercy shall follow me all the days of my life: and I will dwell in the house of the Lord for ever.

PSALM 23:6 KJV

I am not alone, because the Father is with Me.

JOHN 16:32 HCSB

Fear not, for I am with you; Be not dismayed, for I am your God. I will strengthen you.

ISAIAH 41:10 NKJV

MORE BIG IDEAS ABOUT GOD'S PRESENCE

It is enough to know his promise that he will give what is good—he knows so much more about that than we do.

ELISABETH ELLIOT

The tender eyes of God perpetually see us. He has never stopped noticing.

ANGELA THOMAS

A sense of deity is inscribed on every heart.

JOHN CALVIN

God knows that we, with our limited vision, don't even know that for which we should pray. When we entrust our requests to him, we trust him to honor our prayers with holy judgment.

MAX LUCADO

God knows us inside out and outside in. He understands what motivates us and accepts us even in our worst moments.

THELMA WELLS

Our heavenly Father wants nothing but the best for any of us, and only He knows what that is, for He is All-wise, the Omniscient.

ELISABETH ELLIOT

God knows everything. No question can confound Him. No dilemma can confuse Him. No event can surprise Him. He has eternal, intrinsic, comprehensive, and absolutely perfect knowledge.

BILL HYBELS

We may ignore, but we can nowhere evade, the presence of God. The world is crowded with Him. He walks everywhere incognito. And the incognito is not always hard to penetrate. The real labour is to remember, to attend. In fact, to come awake. Still more, to remain awake.

C. S. LEWIS

God possesses infinite knowledge and awareness which is uniquely His. At all times, even in the midst of any type of suffering, I can realize that he knows, loves, watches, understands, and more than that, He has a purpose.

BILLY GRAHAM

The world, space, and all visible
components reverberate
with God's Presence and
demonstrate His Mighty Power.

FRANKLIN GRAHAM

THOUGHTS ABOUT WHAT GOD CAN DO

A PRAYER FOR TODAY

Dear Lord, You are always with me, and You are always listening. Help me feel Your presence in every situation and in every circumstance. Today, Dear God, let me feel the presence of Your love, Your power, and Your Son. Amen

4

GOD CANNOT
WITHHOLD HIS
FORGIVENESS
WHEN YOU
FORGIVE OTHERS

For if you forgive men when they sin against you, your heavenly Father will also forgive you. But if you do not forgive men their sins, your Father will not forgive your sins.

MATTHEW 6:14-15 NIV

THE BIG IDEA

God's forgiveness is real. And, because He has forgiven you, you must forgive others.

YOUR MERCIFUL FATHER

God's power to forgive, like His love, is infinite. Despite your shortcomings, despite your sins, God offers you immediate forgiveness and eternal life when you accept Christ as your Savior.

As a believer who is the recipient of God's forgiveness, how should you behave toward others? Should you forgive them (just as God has forgiven you), or should you remain embittered and resentful? The answer, of course, is found in God's Word: you are instructed to forgive others. When you do, you not only obey God's command, you also free yourself from a prison of your own making.

God offers you immediate forgiveness and eternal life.

When it comes to forgiveness, God doesn't play favorites and neither should you. You should forgive all those who have harmed you (not just the people who have asked for forgiveness or those who have made restitution). Complete forgiveness is God's way, and it should be your way, too. Anything less is an affront to Him and a burden to you.

MORE FROM GOD'S WORD

Praise be to the God and Father of our Lord Jesus Christ! In his great mercy he has given us new birth into a living hope through the resurrection of Jesus Christ from the dead.

1 PETER 1:3 NIV

My soul, praise the Lord, and do not forget all His benefits. He forgives all your sin; He heals all your diseases. He redeems your life from the Pit; He crowns you with faithful love and compassion.

PSALM 103:2-4 HCSB

But God's mercy is great, and he loved us very much. Though we were spiritually dead because of the things we did against God, he gave us new life with Christ. You have been saved by God's grace.

EPHESIANS 2:4-5 NCV

And the LORD said, "I will cause all my goodness to pass in front of you, and I will proclaim my name, the LORD, in your presence. I will have mercy on whom I will have mercy, and I will have compassion on whom I will have compassion."

EXODUS 33:19 NIV

MORE BIG IDEAS ABOUT
GOD'S FORGIVENESS

God expects us to forgive others as He has forgiven us; we are to follow His example by having a forgiving heart.

VONETTE BRIGHT

The pardon of God deletes past, present, and future sins— completely!

FRANKLIN GRAHAM

Because his mercies are new every morning, you can find the courage to bring all of who you are to all of who he is.

SHEILA WALSH

Mistakes offer the possibility for redemption and a new start in God's kingdom. No matter what you're guilty of, God can restore your innocence.

BARBARA JOHNSON

To be righteous means to be in right standing with God because your sins have been taken care of!

KAY ARTHUR

It doesn't matter how big the sin is or how small, it doesn't matter whether it was spontaneous or malicious. God will forgive you if you come to Him and confess your sin!

ANNE GRAHAM LOTZ

Every time we forgive others, deserving it or not, we have a reminder of God's forgiveness.

FRANKLIN GRAHAM

There is nothing that God cannot forgive except for the rejection of Christ. No matter how black the sin, how hideous the sin, if we but confess it to Him in true repentance and faith, He will forgive. He will accept and forgive.

RUTH BELL GRAHAM

It stands to reason that if Jesus asked His Father to forgive the very men who crucified Him, and God did, then there is nothing and no one that He cannot or will not forgive when He is humbly asked.

ANNE GRAHAM LOTZ

There is only One
who can cleanse us from our sins—
He who made us.

—

CORRIE TEN BOOM

THOUGHTS ABOUT WHAT GOD CAN DO

A PRAYER FOR TODAY

Dear Lord, You have given me so much more than I deserve. You have blessed me with Your love and Your mercy. Help me be merciful toward others, Father, just as You have been merciful toward me, and let me share Your love with a world that desperately needs Your mercy and Your Son. Amen

5

GOD CANNOT WITHHOLD HIS PROTECTION WHEN YOU ASK FOR IT

Cast your burden on the Lord,
and He shall sustain you; He shall never
permit the righteous to be moved.

—

PSALM 55:22 NKJV

THE BIG IDEA

Your only real security comes from
the loving heart of God—and from
the salvation that flows from
His only begotten Son.

ULTIMATE PROTECTION

Being a godly believer in this difficult world is no easy task. Ours is a time of uncertainty and danger, a time when even the most courageous have legitimate cause for concern. But as believers we can live courageously, knowing that we have been saved by a loving Father and His only begotten Son.

God's Word is the ultimate truth.

In a world filled with more frustrations than we can count, God's Son offers the ultimate peace. In a world filled with dangers and temptations, God is the ultimate armor. In a world filled with misleading messages, God's Word is the ultimate truth.

Will you accept God's peace and wear God's armor against the dangers of our world? And will you acknowledge that God's protection is sufficient for your every need? Hopefully so, because when you do, you can live courageously, knowing that you possess the ultimate protection: God's unfailing love for you.

MORE FROM GOD'S WORD

I know whom I have believed and am persuaded that He is able to guard what has been entrusted to me until that day.

2 TIMOTHY 1:12 HCSB

For the LORD your God has arrived to live among you. He is a mighty savior. He will rejoice over you with great gladness. With his love, he will calm all your fears. He will exult over you by singing a happy song.

ZEPHANIAH 3:17 HCSB

God—His way is perfect; the word of the Lord is pure. He is a shield to all who take refuge in Him.

PSALM 18:30 HCSB

The Lord is my rock, my fortress, and my deliverer.

PSALM 18:2 HCSB

The Lord bless you and protect you; the Lord make His face shine on you, and be gracious to you.

NUMBERS 6:24-25 HCSB

MORE BIG IDEAS ABOUT GOD'S PROTECTION

Under heaven's lock and key, we are protected by the most efficient security system available: the power of God.

CHARLES SWINDOLL

In all the old castles of England, there was a place called the keep. It was always the strongest and best protected place in the castle, and in it were hidden all who were weak and helpless and unable to defend themselves in times of danger. Shall we be afraid to hide ourselves in the keeping power of our Divine Keeper, who neither slumbers nor sleeps, and who has promised to preserve our going out and our coming in, from this time forth and even forever more?

HANNAH WHITALL SMITH

There is not only fear, but terrible danger, for the life unguarded by God.

OSWALD CHAMBERS

He is within and without. His Spirit dwells within me. His armor protects me. He goes before me and is behind me.

MARY MORRISON SUGGS

Through the storm, through the night / Lead me on to the light / Take my hand precious lord, lead me home.

THOMAS A. DORSEY

The Rock of Ages is the great sheltering encirclement.

OSWALD CHAMBERS

The promises of God's Word sustain us in our suffering, and we know Jesus sympathizes and empathizes with us in our darkest hour.

BILL BRIGHT

God delights in spreading His protective wings and enfolding His frightened, weary, beaten-down, worn-out children.

BILL HYBELS

Our responsibility is to feed from Him, to stay close to Him, to follow Him—because sheep easily go astray—so that we eternally experience the protection and companionship of our Great Shepherd the Lord Jesus Christ.

FRANKLIN GRAHAM

There is no safer place to live
than the center of His will.

—

CALVIN MILLER

THOUGHTS ABOUT WHAT GOD CAN DO

A PRAYER FOR TODAY

Lord, You are my Shepherd. You care for me; You comfort me; You watch over me; and You have saved me. I will praise You, Father, for Your glorious works, for Your protection, for Your love, and for Your Son. Amen

6

GOD CANNOT REMEMBER YOUR SINS

It is I who sweep away your transgressions
for My own sake and remember
your sins no more.

—

ISAIAH 43:25 HCSB

THE BIG IDEA

Every day of your life, you will be tempted
to rebel against God's teachings. Your job,
simply put, is to guard your heart against
the darkness as you focus on the light.

HE WIPES THE SLATE CLEAN

Allof us have sinned. Sometimes our sins result from our own stubborn rebellion against God's commandments. Sometimes, we are swept up by events that encourage us to behave in ways that we later come to regret. And sometimes, even when our intentions are honorable, we make mistakes that have long-lasting consequences. When we look back at our actions with remorse, we may experience intense feelings of guilt. But God has an answer for the guilt that we feel. That answer, of course, is His forgiveness.

When we genuinely repent from our wrongdoings, and when we sincerely confess our sins, God not only forgives our shortcomings, He forgets them! But long after God has forgiven us, we may continue to withhold forgiveness from ourselves. Instead of accepting God's mercy and accepting our past, we may think long and hard—far too long and hard—about the things that "might have been," the things that "could have been," or the things that "should have been."

Once God has forgiven you, you should forgive yourself, too.

Are you troubled by feelings of guilt, even after you've received God's forgiveness? Are you still struggling with painful memories of mistakes you made long ago? Are you focused so intently on yesterday that your vision of today is clouded? If so you still have work to do—spiritual work. You should ask your Heavenly Father not for forgiveness (He granted that gift the very first time you asked Him!) but instead for acceptance and trust: acceptance of the past and trust in God's plan for your life.

Once you have asked God for His forgiveness, you can be certain that your Heavenly Father has given it. And if He, in His infinite wisdom, is willing to forgive your sins and forget them, how then can you withhold forgiveness from yourself? The answer, of course, is that once God has forgiven you, you should forgive yourself, too.

When you forgive yourself thoroughly and completely, you'll stop investing energy in those most useless of emotions: bitterness, regret, and self-recrimination. And you can then get busy making the world a better place, and that's as it should be. After all, since God has forgiven you, isn't it about time that you demonstrate your gratitude by serving Him?

MORE FROM GOD'S WORD

Heaven and earth will pass away, but My words will never pass away.

MATTHEW 24:35 HCSB

But God, who is abundant in mercy, because of His great love that He had for us, made us alive with the Messiah even though we were dead in trespasses. By grace you are saved!

EPHESIANS 2:4-5 HCSB

My grace is sufficient for you, for My strength is made perfect in weakness.

2 CORINTHIANS 12:9 NKJV

In Him we have redemption through His blood, the forgiveness of our trespasses, according to the riches of His grace that He lavished on us with all wisdom and understanding.

EPHESIANS 1:7-8 HCSB

But the word of the Lord endures forever. And this is the word that was preached as the gospel to you.

1 PETER 1:25 HCSB

MORE BIG IDEAS ABOUT NEW BEGINNINGS

Mistakes offer the possibility for redemption and a new start in God's kingdom. No matter what you're guilty of, God can restore your innocence.

BARBARA JOHNSON

Walking with God leads to receiving his intimate counsel, and counseling leads to deep restoration.

JOHN ELDREDGE

God is not running an antique shop! He is making all things new!

VANCE HAVNER

The amazing thing about Jesus is that He doesn't just patch up our lives, He gives us a brand new sheet, a clean slate to start over, all new.

GLORIA GAITHER

Like a spring of pure water, God's peace in our hearts brings cleansing and refreshment to our minds and bodies.

BILLY GRAHAM

Whoever you are, whatever your condition or circumstance, whatever your past or problem, Jesus can restore you to wholeness.

ANNE GRAHAM LOTZ

Walking with God leads to receiving his intimate counsel, and counseling leads to deep restoration.

JOHN ELDREDGE

No matter how badly we have failed, we can always get up and begin again. Our God is the God of new beginnings.

WARREN WIERSBE

Troubles we bear trustfully can bring us a fresh vision of God and a new outlook on life, an outlook of peace and hope.

BILLY GRAHAM

The same voice that brought Lazarus out of the tomb raised us to newness of life.

C. H. SPURGEON

When we focus on God, the scene changes. He's in control of our lives; nothing lies outside the realm of His redemptive grace. Even when we make mistakes, fail in relationships, or deliberately make bad choices, God can redeem us.

—

PENELOPE J. STOKES

THOUGHTS ABOUT WHAT GOD CAN DO

A PRAYER FOR TODAY

Dear Lord, I am an imperfect human being. When I have sinned, let me repent from my wrongdoings, and let me seek forgiveness—first from You, then from others, and finally from myself. Amen

7

GOD CANNOT DISTANCE HIMSELF FROM YOU WHEN YOU CALL UPON HIM

The Lord is near to all who call upon Him,
to all who call upon Him in truth.
He will fulfill the desire of those who fear Him;
He also will hear their cry and save them.
The Lord preserves all who love Him.

—

PSALM 145:18-20 NKJV

THE BIG IDEA

Whatever you need, God can provide.
He is always sufficient to meet your needs.

HE WILL NEVER FAIL YOU

God has promised to lift you up and guide your steps if you let Him do so. God has promised that when you entrust your life to Him completely and without reservation, He will give you the strength to meet any challenge, the courage to face any trial, and the wisdom to live in His righteousness. These, by the way, are promises that the Lord will surely keep.

God will hold your hand and walk with you every day of your life if you let Him. So even if your circumstances are difficult, trust the Father. His love is eternal and His goodness endures forever.

Today, remember that God's hand uplifts those who turn their hearts and prayers to Him. Accept God's peace and wear His armor

God will give you the strength to meet any challenge.

against the temptations and distractions of this dangerous world. And while you're at it, be mindful of this fact: the loving heart of God is sufficient to meet any challenge . . . including yours.

MORE FROM GOD'S WORD

The LORD is my strength and song, and He has become my salvation; He is my God, and I will praise Him . . . .

EXODUS 15:2 NKJV

But my God shall supply all your need according to his riches in glory by Christ Jesus.

PHILIPPIANS 4:19 KJV

The Lord is my rock, my fortress and my savior; my God is my rock in whom I find protection. He is my shield, the strength of my salvation, and my stronghold.

PSALM 18:2 NLT

The Lord says, "I will rescue those who love me. I will protect those who trust in my name."

PSALM 91:14 NLT

So, what do you think? With God on our side like this, how can we lose? If God didn't hesitate to put everything on the line for us, embracing our condition and exposing himself to the worst by sending his own Son, is there anything else he wouldn't gladly and freely do for us?

ROMANS 8:31-32 MSG

MORE BIG IDEAS ABOUT GOD'S SUPPORT

God is always sufficient in perfect proportion to our need.

BETH MOORE

God is great and God is powerful, but we must invite him to be powerful in our lives. His strength is always there, but it's up to us to provide a channel through which that power can flow.

BILL HYBELS

God uses our most stumbling, faltering faith-steps as the open door to His doing for us "more than we ask or think."

CATHERINE MARSHALL

Faith is not merely you holding on to God—it is God holding on to you.

E. STANLEY JONES

Whatever may be our circumstances in life, may each one of us really believe that by way of the Throne we have unlimited power.

ANNIE ARMSTRONG

He stands fast as your rock, steadfast as your safeguard, sleepless as your watcher, valiant as your champion.

C. H. SPURGEON

Once we recognize our need for Jesus, then the building of our faith begins. It is a daily, moment-by-moment life of absolute dependence upon Him for everything.

CATHERINE MARSHALL

Measure the size of the obstacles against the size of God.

BETH MOORE

The last and greatest lesson that the soul has to learn is the fact that God, and God alone, is enough for all its needs. This is the lesson that all His dealings with us are meant to teach; and this is the crowning discovery of our whole Christian life. God is enough!

HANNAH WHITALL SMITH

God will never lead you where His strength cannot keep you.

BARBARA JOHNSON

Snuggle in God's arms.
When you are hurting,
when you feel lonely or left out,
let Him cradle you, comfort you,
reassure you of His all-sufficient
power and love.

—

KAY ARTHUR

THOUGHTS ABOUT WHAT GOD CAN DO

A PRAYER FOR TODAY

Heavenly Father, You never leave or forsake me. You are always with me, protecting me and encouraging me. Whatever this day may bring, I thank You for Your love and Your strength. Let me lean upon You, Father, this day and forever. Amen

8

GOD CANNOT
IGNORE YOUR
ACTIONS,
AND HE CANNOT
REFRAIN FROM
JUDGING THEM

For God will bring every act to judgment,
including every hidden thing,
whether good or evil.

—

ECCLESIASTES 12:14 HCSB

THE BIG IDEA

God is always watching over you,
and He has created a universe in which
actions have consequences.
God rewards righteousness and punishes sin,
so please behave accordingly.

BECAUSE GOD IS JUST,
WE MUSE CHOOSE WISELY

Life is a series of choices. Each day, we make countless decisions that can bring us closer to God . . . or not. When we live according to God's commandments, we earn for ourselves the abundance and peace that He intends for our lives. But, when we turn our backs upon God by ignoring Him—or by disobeying Him—we bring needless pain and suffering upon ourselves and our families.

Do you want God's peace and His blessings? Then obey Him. When you're faced with a difficult choice or a powerful

Seek God's counsel and trust the counsel He gives.

temptation, seek God's counsel and trust the counsel He gives. Invite God into your heart and live according to His commandments. And when God speaks to you through that little quiet voice that He has placed in your heart, listen. When you do, you will be blessed today, and tomorrow, and forever. And you'll discover that happiness means living in accordance with your beliefs. No exceptions.

MORE FROM GOD'S WORD

Every man's way is right in his own eyes, but the LORD weighs the hearts.

PROVERBS 21:2 NASB

I am He who searches the minds and hearts. And I will give to each one of you according to your works.

REVELATION 2:23 NKJV

As for myself, I do not care if I am judged by you or by any human court. I do not even judge myself. I know of no wrong I have done, but this does not make me right before the Lord. The Lord is the One who judges me.

1 CORINTHIANS 4:3-4 NCV

I assure you: Anyone who hears My word and believes Him who sent Me has eternal life and will not come under judgment, but has passed from death to life.

JOHN 5:24 HCSB

In Him we have redemption through His blood, the forgiveness of our trespasses, according to the riches of His grace that He lavished on us with all wisdom and understanding.

EPHESIANS 1:7-8 HCSB

MORE BIG IDEAS ABOUT GOD'S JUDGMENT

Some day we will stand before God. And when we do, we will need something more than speculative imagination or a warm, fuzzy feeling.

CHARLES SWINDOLL

My conscience is captive to the word of God.

MARTIN LUTHER

Every secret act of character, conviction, and courage has been observed in living color by our omniscient God.

BILL HYBELS

It is comfortable to know that we are responsible to God and not to man. It is a small matter to be judged of man's judgement.

LOTTIE MOON

The convicting work of the Holy Spirit awakens, disturbs, and judges.

FRANKLIN GRAHAM

God's curriculum for all who sincerely want to know Him and do His will always includes lessons we wish we could skip. With an intimate understanding of our deepest needs and individual capacities, He chooses our curriculum.

ELISABETH ELLIOT

The kingdom of God is a kingdom of paradox where, through the ugly defeat of a cross, a holy God is utterly glorified. Victory comes through defeat; healing through brokenness; finding self through losing self.

CHUCK COLSON

Recently I've been learning that life comes down to this: God is in everything. Regardless of what difficulties I am experiencing at the moment, or what things aren't as I would like them to be, I look at the circumstances and say, "Lord, what are you trying to teach me?"

CATHERINE MARSHALL

Our battles are first won or lost in the secret places of our will in God's presence, never in full view of the world.

OSWALD CHAMBERS

God is the only judge.
You are just his emissary of peace.
—

ST. THÉRÈSE OF LISIEUX

THOUGHTS ABOUT WHAT GOD CAN DO

A PRAYER FOR TODAY

Dear Lord, Your love is eternal and Your laws are everlasting. When I obey Your commandments, I am blessed. Today, I invite You to reign over every corner of my heart. I will have faith in You, Father. I will sense Your presence; I will accept Your love; I will trust Your will; and I will praise You for the Savior of my life: Your Son Jesus. Amen

9

GOD CANNOT
DEPRIVE YOU
OF SPIRITUAL
ABUNDANCE

I am come that they might have life,
and that they might have it more abundantly.

—

JOHN 10:10 KJV

THE BIG IDEA

God will provide for your needs if you stay
focused on doing His will. He wants you to
experience the kind of spiritual abundance
that only He can provide.

GOD WILL NOT WITHHOLD
HIS ABUNDANCE

The Word of God is clear: Christ came in order that we might have life abundant and life eternal. Eternal life is the priceless possession of all who invite Christ into their hearts, but God's abundance is optional: He does not force it upon us.

When we entrust our hearts and our days to the One who created us, we experience abundance through the grace and sacrifice of His Son. But, when we turn our thoughts and direct our energies away from God's commandments, we inevitably forfeit the spiritual abundance that might otherwise be ours.

Do you sincerely seek the riches that our Savior offers to those who give themselves to Him? Then follow Him completely and obey Him without reservation. When you do, you will receive the love and the abundance that He has

> **We experience abundance through the grace and sacrifice of His Son.**

promised. Seek first the salvation that is available through a personal relationship with Jesus Christ, and then claim the joy, the peace, and the spiritual abundance that the Shepherd offers His sheep.

MORE FROM GOD'S WORD

And God is able to make every grace overflow to you, so that in every way, always having everything you need, you may excel in every good work.

2 CORINTHIANS 9:8 HCSB

Until now you have asked for nothing in My name. Ask and you will receive, that your joy may be complete.

JOHN 16:24 HCSB

Come to terms with God and be at peace; in this way good will come to you.

JOB 22:21 HCSB

My cup runs over. Surely goodness and mercy shall follow me all the days of my life; and I will dwell in the house of the Lord forever.

PSALM 23:5-6 NKJV

And He said to them, "Take heed and beware of covetousness, for one's life does not consist in the abundance of the things he possesses."

LUKE 12:15 NKJV

MORE BIG IDEAS ABOUT
SPIRITUAL ABUNDANCE

God's riches are beyond anything we could ask or even dare to imagine! If my life gets stale, I have no excuse.

BARBARA JOHNSON

Grow, dear friends, but grow, I beg you, in God's way, which is the only true way.

HANNAH WHITALL SMITH

Jesus wants Life for us, Life with a capital L.

JOHN ELDREDGE

God is the giver, and we are the receivers. And His richest gifts are bestowed not upon those who do the greatest things, but upon those who accept His abundance and His grace.

HANNAH WHITALL SMITH

The only way you can experience abundant life is to surrender your plans to Him.

CHARLES STANLEY

God has promised us abundance, peace, and eternal life. These treasures are ours for the asking; all we must do is claim them. One of the great mysteries of life is why on earth do so many of us wait so very long to lay claim to God's gifts?

MARIE T. FREEMAN

In the kingdom of God, the surest way to lose something is to try to protect it, and the best way to keep it is to let it go.

A. W. TOZER

We set our eyes on the finish line, forgetting the past, and straining toward the mark of spiritual maturity and fruitfulness.

VONETTE BRIGHT

God loves you and wants you to experience peace and life—abundant and eternal.

BILLY GRAHAM

Jesus intended for us to be
overwhelmed by the blessings
of regular days. He said it was
the reason he had come:
"I am come that they might have
life, and that they might have it
more abundantly."

GLORIA GAITHER

THOUGHTS ABOUT WHAT GOD CAN DO

A PRAYER FOR TODAY

Heavenly Father, You have promised an abundant life through Your Son Jesus. Thank You, Lord, for Your abundance. Guide me according to Your will, so that I might be a worthy servant in all that I say and do, this day and every day. Amen

10

GOD CANNOT
IGNORE YOUR
TROUBLES

The Lord is a shelter for the oppressed,
a refuge in times of trouble. Those who know
your name trust in you, for you,
O LORD, have never abandoned anyone
who searches for you.

PSALM 9:9-10 NLT

THE BIG IDEA

When tough times arrive, you should
work as if everything depended on you and
pray as if everything depended on God.

ENDURING TOUGH TIMES

From time to time, all of us face adversity, hardship, disappointment, and loss. Old Man Trouble pays periodic visits to each of us; none of us are exempt. When we are troubled, God stands ready and willing to protect us. Our responsibility, of course, is to ask Him for protection. When we call upon Him in heartfelt prayer, He will answer—in His own time and in accordance with His own perfect plan.

Our world continues to change, but God's love remains constant. And, He remains ready to comfort us and strengthen us whenever we turn to Him. Psalm 145 promises, "The Lord is near to all who call on him, to all who call on him in truth. He fulfills the desires of those who fear him; he hears their cry and saves them" (vv. 18-20 NIV).

> **When we call upon Him in heartfelt prayer, He will answer.**

Life is often challenging, but as Christians, we must not be afraid. God loves us, and He will protect us. In times of hardship, He will comfort us; in times of sorrow, He will dry our tears. When we are troubled, or weak, or sorrowful, God is always with us. We must build our lives on the rock that cannot be shaken . . . we must trust in God. Always.

MORE FROM GOD'S WORD

We also have joy with our troubles, because we know that these troubles produce patience. And patience produces character, and character produces hope.

ROMANS 5:3-4 NCV

Be strong and courageous. Do not be terrified; do not be discouraged, for the LORD your God will be with you wherever you go.

JOSHUA 1:9 NIV

You pulled me from the brink of death, my feet from the cliff-edge of doom. Now I stroll at leisure with God in the sunlit fields of life.

PSALM 56:13 MSG

Don't fret or worry. Instead of worrying, pray. Let petitions and praises shape your worries into prayers, letting God know your concerns. Before you know it, a sense of God's wholeness, everything coming together for good, will come and settle you down. It's wonderful what happens when Christ displaces worry at the center of your life.

PHILIPPIANS 4:6-7 MSG

MORE BIG IDEAS ABOUT TOUGH TIMES

Times of travail can be times of birth. Today's suffering can mean tomorrow's glory.

WARREN WIERSBE

In order to realize the worth of the anchor, we need to feel the stress of the storm.

CORRIE TEN BOOM

This hard place in which you perhaps find yourself is the very place in which God is giving you opportunity to look only to Him, to spend time in prayer, and to learn long-suffering, gentleness, meekness—in short, to learn the depths of the love that Christ Himself has poured out on all of us.

ELISABETH ELLIOT

Oh, remember this: There is never a time when we may not hope in God. Whatever our necessities, however great our difficulties, and though to all appearance, help is impossible, yet our business is to hope in God, and it will be found that it is not in vain.

GEORGE MUELLER

Any man can sing in the day. It is easy to sing when we can read the notes by daylight, but he is the skillful singer who can sing when there is not a ray of light by which to read. Songs in the night come only from God; they are not in the power of man.

C. H. SPURGEON

Speak the name of "Jesus," and all your storms will fold their thunderbolts and leave.

CALVIN MILLER

The hope we have in Jesus is the anchor for the soul— something sure and steadfast, preventing drifting or giving way, lowered to the depth of God's love.

FRANKLIN GRAHAM

If your every human plan and calculation has miscarried, if, one by one, human props have been knocked out . . . take heart. God is trying to get a message through to you, and the message is: "Stop depending on inadequate human resources. Let me handle the matter."

CATHERINE MARSHALL

The only thing more tragic than
the tragedy that happens to us
is the way we handle it.

—

JOHN ELDREDGE

THOUGHTS ABOUT WHAT GOD CAN DO

A PRAYER FOR TODAY

Heavenly Father, You are my strength and my refuge. As I journey through this day, I know that I may encounter disappointments and losses. When I am troubled, let me turn to You. Keep me steady, Lord, and renew a right spirit inside of me this day and forever. Amen

11

GOD CANNOT ALLOW YOU TO ENCOUNTER IRRESISTIBLE TEMPTATIONS

*No temptation has overtaken you except
what is common to humanity. God is faithful
and He will not allow you to be tempted beyond
what you are able, but with the temptation
He will also provide a way of escape,
so that you are able to bear it.*

—

1 CORINTHIANS 10:13 HCSB

THE BIG IDEA

You live in a temptation-filled world. God
won't allow you to experience more of those
temptations than you can bear, but you, too,
must do your part to resist them.

NO TEMPTATION TOO GREAT

It's inevitable: today you will be tempted by somebody or something—in fact, you will probably be tempted on countless occasions. Why? Because you live in a world that's filled to the brim with temptations and addictions that are intended to grab your attention, your money, and ultimately your life.

Here in the 21st century, temptations are now completely and thoroughly woven into the fabric of everyday life. Seductive images are everywhere; subtle messages tell you that it's okay to sin "just a little"; and to make matters even worse, society doesn't just seem to endorse godlessness, it actually seems to reward it. Society spews forth a wide range of messages, all of which imply that it's okay to rebel against God's Word. These messages, of course, are extremely dangerous and completely untrue.

> **God has promised that with His help, you can resist every single temptation that confronts you.**

How can you stand up against society's tidal wave of temptations? By learning to direct your thoughts and your eyes toward things that are pleasing to God . . . and by relying upon Him to help you stay focused on "whatever is honorable, whatever is just, whatever is pure, whatever is lovely, whatever is commendable" (Philippians 4:8). And here's the good news: the Creator has promised (not implied, not suggested, not insinuated—He has promised!) that with His help, you can resist every single temptation that confronts you (1 Corinthians 10:13).

Once you firmly decide to stand up to temptation, you are never alone. God is always with you, and if you do your part He will do His part. But what, precisely, is your part? A good starting point is simply learning how to recognize the subtle temptations that surround—and assault—you. The images of immorality are ubiquitous, and they're intended to hijack your mind, your heart, your wallet, and your soul. Don't let them do it.

We pursue righteousness when we flee
the things that keep us from
following the Lord Jesus.
These are the keys: flee, follow, and fight.

—

FRANKLIN GRAHAM

MORE FROM GOD'S WORD

Do not be deceived: "Bad company corrupts good morals."
1 CORINTHIANS 15:33 HCSB

Be sober! Be on the alert! Your adversary the Devil is prowling around like a roaring lion, looking for anyone he can devour.
1 PETER 5:8 HCSB

The Lord knows how to deliver the godly out of temptations.
2 PETER 2:9 NKJV

Put on the full armor of God so that you can stand against the tactics of the Devil.
EPHESIANS 6:11 HCSB

For we do not have a High Priest who cannot sympathize with our weaknesses, but was in all points tempted as we are, yet without sin. Let us therefore come boldly to the throne of grace, that we may obtain mercy and find grace to help in time of need.
HEBREWS 4:15-16 NKJV

MORE BIG IDEAS ABOUT TEMPTATION

Do not fight the temptation in detail. Turn from it. Look ONLY at your Lord. Sing. Read. Work.

AMY CARMICHAEL

Instant intimacy is one of the leading warning signals of a seduction.

BETH MOORE

Our Lord has given us an example of how to overcome the devil's temptations. When he was tempted in the wilderness, He defeated Satan every time by the use of the Bible.

BILLY GRAHAM

Temptation is not a sin. Even Jesus was tempted. The Lord Jesus gives you the strength needed to resist temptation.

CORRIE TEN BOOM

The higher the hill, the stronger the wind: so the loftier the life, the stronger the enemy's temptations.

JOHN WYCLIFFE

The Bible teaches us in times of temptation there is one command: Flee! Get away from it, for every struggle against lust using only one's own strength is doomed to failure.

DIETRICH BONHOEFFER

Every time we are tempted in life, it will be by something immediate. It will be something that will suggest to us that we need to postpone the more important for the more urgent.

FRANKLIN GRAHAM

Sin is an allergic reaction to God's law, an irrational anti-God syndrome that drives us to exalt ourselves and steels our heart against devotion and obedience to our Maker.

J. I. PACKER

Take a really honest look at yourself. Have any old sins begun to take control again? This would be a wonderful time to allow Him to bring fresh order out of longstanding chaos.

CHARLES SWINDOLL

THOUGHTS ABOUT WHAT GOD CAN DO

A PRAYER FOR TODAY

Dear Lord, this world is filled with temptations, distractions, and frustrations. When I turn my thoughts away from You and Your Word, Lord, I suffer bitter consequences. But, when I trust in Your commandments, I am safe. Direct my path far from the temptations and distractions of the world. Let me discover Your will and follow it, Lord, this day and always. Amen

12

GOD CANNOT SPONSOR A FAILURE

*Now thanks be to God who always leads us
in triumph in Christ.*

—

2 CORINTHIANS 2:14 HCSB

THE BIG IDEA

Success according to God requires
perseverance, prayer, and patience—
if you want to be successful,
you'll need all three.

SUCCESS ACCORDING TO GOD

How do you define success? Do you define it as the accumulation of material possessions or the adulation of your neighbors? If so, you need to reorder your priorities. Genuine success has little to do with fame or fortune; it has everything to do with God's gift of love and His promise of salvation.

If you have welcomed God into your heart, you are already a towering success, but there is still more that you can do. Your task—as a person who has been touched by the Creator's grace—is to accept the spiritual abundance and peace He offers to those who trust His promises. Then, you can share the healing message of God's love and His abundance with a world that desperately needs both. When you do, you will have reached the pinnacle of success.

> **Genuine success has little to do with fame or fortune; it has everything to do with God's gifts.**

MORE FROM GOD'S WORD

Take delight in the Lord, and He will give you your heart's desires.

PSALM 37:4 HCSB

The one who acquires good sense loves himself; one who safeguards understanding finds success.

PROVERBS 19:8 HCSB

The one who understands a matter finds success, and the one who trusts in the Lord will be happy.

PROVERBS 16:20 HCSB

Remember this: the person who sows sparingly will also reap sparingly, and the person who sows generously will also reap generously.

2 CORINTHIANS 9:6 HCSB

Believe in the Lord your God, and you will be established; believe in His prophets, and you will succeed.

2 CHRONICLES 20:20 HCSB

MORE BIG IDEAS ABOUT SUCCESS

There's not much you can't achieve or endure if you know God is walking by your side. Just remember: Someone knows, and Someone cares.

BILL HYBELS

We, as believers, must allow God to define success. And, when we do, God blesses us with His love and His grace.

JIM GALLERY

Success or failure can be pretty well predicted by the degree to which the heart is fully in it.

JOHN ELDREDGE

Often, attitude is the only difference between success and failure.

JOHN MAXWELL

Success and happiness are not destinations. They are exciting, never-ending journeys.

ZIG ZIGLAR

We have a God who delights in impossibilities.

ANDREW MURRAY

God provides the ingredients for our daily bread but expects us to do the baking. With our own hands!

BARBARA JOHNSON

Never forget: If you belong to the King, you are on the winning side.

BILLY GRAHAM

The story of every great Christian achievement is the history of answered prayer.

E. M. BOUNDS

To be successful, you can't just run on the fast track: run on your track.

JOHN MAXWELL

Success or failure can be pretty well predicted by the degree to which the heart is fully in it.

JOHN ELDREDGE

You can't climb the ladder of life
with your hands in your pockets.

—

BARBARA JOHNSON

THOUGHTS ABOUT WHAT GOD CAN DO

_____

_____

_____

_____

_____

_____

_____

_____

_____

_____

A PRAYER FOR TODAY

Dear Lord, let Your plans be my plans. Let Your will be my will. And let Your Word be my guide as I focus, not on the world's approval, but on Your approval. Amen

13

GOD CANNOT WITHHOLD HIS GUIDANCE WHEN YOU TRUST HIM

Trust in the Lord with all your heart,
and lean not on your own understanding;
in all your ways acknowledge Him,
and He shall direct your paths.

—

PROVERBS 3:5-6 NKJV

THE BIG IDEA

When you pray for guidance,
God will give it.
If you're wise, you'll allow God to guide you
today and every day of your life.

HE HAS PROMISED TO GUIDE YOU

When we genuinely seek to know God's will—when we prayerfully seek His wisdom and His guidance—our Heavenly Father carefully leads us over the peaks and valleys of life. And as Christians, we can be comforted: Whether we find ourselves at the pinnacle of the mountain or the darkest depths of the valley, God is always there with us.

C. S. Lewis observed, "I don't doubt that the Holy Spirit guides your decisions from within when you make them with the intention of pleasing God. The error would be to think that He speaks only within, whereas in reality He speaks also through Scripture,

Lean upon God's promises and lift your prayers to Him.

the Church, Christian friends, and books." These words remind us that God has many ways to make Himself known. Our challenge is to make ourselves open to His instruction.

Do you place a high value on God's guidance, and do you talk to Him regularly about matters great and small? Or do you talk with God on a haphazard basis? If you're wise, you'll form the habit of speaking to God early and often. But you won't stop there—you'll also study God's Word, you'll obey God's commandments, and you'll associate with people who do likewise.

So, if you're unsure of your next step, lean upon God's promises and lift your prayers to Him. Remember that God is always near—always trying to get His message through. Open yourself to Him every day, and trust Him to guide your path. When you do, you'll be protected today, tomorrow, and forever.

As God's children, we are the recipients of lavish love—a love that motivates us to keep trusting even when we have no idea what God is doing.

BETH MOORE

MORE FROM GOD'S WORD

Then you will know that I am the Lord; those who put their hope in Me will not be put to shame.

ISAIAH 49:23 HCSB

For the Lord God is our light and our protector. He gives us grace and glory. No good thing will the Lord withhold from those who do what is right. O Lord Almighty, happy are those who trust in you.

PSALM 84:11-12 NLT

Trust ye in the LORD for ever: for in the LORD JEHOVAH is everlasting strength.

ISAIAH 26:4 KJV

Let us hold fast the confession of our hope without wavering, for He who promised is faithful.

HEBREWS 10:23 NKJV

The LORD is my rock, and my fortress, and my deliverer; my God, my strength, in whom I will trust....

PSALM 18:2 KJV

MORE BIG IDEAS ABOUT TRUSTING GOD

God is God. He knows what he is doing. When you can't trace his hand, trust his heart.

MAX LUCADO

Do not be afraid, then, that if you trust, or tell others to trust, the matter will end there. Trust is only the beginning and the continual foundation. When we trust Him, the Lord works, and His work is the important part of the whole matter.

HANNAH WHITALL SMITH

Faith does not eliminate problems. Faith keeps you in a trusting relationship with God in the midst of your problems.

HENRY BLACKABY

Are you serious about wanting God's guidance to become the person he wants you to be? The first step is to tell God that you know you can't manage your own life; that you need his help.

CATHERINE MARSHALL

Beware of trusting in yourself, and see that you trust in the Lord.

OSWALD CHAMBERS

The hope we have in Jesus is the anchor for the soul—something sure and steadfast, preventing drifting or giving way, lowered to the depth of God's love.

FRANKLIN GRAHAM

Trustfulness is based on confidence in God whose ways I do not understand.

OSWALD CHAMBERS

Sometimes the very essence of faith is trusting God in the midst of things He knows good and well we cannot comprehend.

BETH MOORE

Never be afraid to trust an unknown future to a known God.

CORRIE TEN BOOM

THOUGHTS ABOUT WHAT GOD CAN DO

A PRAYER FOR TODAY

*Lord, give me courage in every circumstance and in every stage
of life. Give me the wisdom, Father, to place my hope and my
trust in Your perfect plan and Your boundless love. Amen*

14

GOD CANNOT
BE UNFAITHFUL

Praise the Lord, all nations!
Glorify Him, all peoples!
For great is His faithful love to us;
the Lord's faithfulness endures forever.
Hallelujah!

—

PSALM 117 HCSB

THE BIG IDEA

God's faithfulness is steadfast,
unwavering, and eternal.

HE IS FAITHFUL

God can never be unfaithful. In fact, He is faithful to us even when we are not faithful to Him. God keeps His promises to us even when we stray far from His will. He continues to love us even when we disobey His commandments. But, one thing God does not do is this: He doesn't force His blessings upon us. If we are to experience His love and His grace, we must claim them for ourselves.

Are you tired, discouraged, or fearful? Be comforted: God is with you. Are you confused? Listen prayerfully to the quiet voice of your Heavenly Father. Are you bitter? Talk with God and seek His guidance. Are you engaged in behavior that is contrary to God's will? Ask God to help guide you in the footsteps of His Son. Remember that God is always faithful to you . . . and you, in turn, must be faithful to Him.

God keeps His promises to us even when we stray.

MORE FROM GOD'S WORD

If we confess our sins, He is faithful and just to forgive us our sins and to cleanse us from all unrighteousness.

1 JOHN 1:9 NKJV

For the eyes of the Lord range throughout the earth to show Himself strong for those whose hearts are completely His.

2 CHRONICLES 16:9 HCSB

Those who trust in the LORD are as secure as Mount Zion; they will not be defeated but will endure forever.

PSALM 125:1 NLT

The Good News shows how God makes people right with himself—that it begins and ends with faith. As the Scripture says, "But those who are right with God will live by trusting in him."

ROMANS 1:17 NCV

Trust in the LORD with all your heart; do not depend on your own understanding. Seek his will in all you do, and he will direct your paths.

PROVERBS 3:5-6 NLT

MORE BIG IDEAS ABOUT
GOD'S FAITHFULNESS

It is a joy that God never abandons His children. He guides faithfully all who listen to His directions.

CORRIE TEN BOOM

God's faithfulness and grace make the impossible possible.

SHEILA WALSH

God does not want to be a divine lifeguard who is summoned only in emergencies. He wants to be involved in every aspect of our lives.

WARREN WIERSBE

With each new experience of letting God be in control, we gain courage and reinforcement for daring to do it again and again.

GLORIA GAITHER

God is my heavenly Father. He loves me with an everlasting love. The proof of that is the Cross.

ELISABETH ELLIOT

By ourselves we are not capable of suffering bravely, but the Lord possesses all the strength we lack and will demonstrate His power when we undergo persecution.

CORRIE TEN BOOM

And in truth, if we only knew it, our chief fitness is our utter helplessness. His strength is made perfect, not in our strength, but in our weakness. Our strength is only a hindrance.

HANNAH WHITALL SMITH

Grace comes from the heart of a gracious God who wants to stun you and overwhelm you with a gift you don't deserve—salvation, adoption, a spiritual ability to use in kingdom service, answered prayer, the church, His presence, His wisdom, His guidance, His love.

BILL HYBELS

Walk in the daylight of God's will because then you will be safe; you will not stumble.

ANNE GRAHAM LOTZ

God expresses His love toward us
by His uninterrupted presence
in our lives.

—

CHARLES STANLEY

THOUGHTS ABOUT WHAT GOD CAN DO

_____

_____

_____

_____

_____

_____

_____

_____

_____

_____

A PRAYER FOR TODAY

Thank You, Dear Lord, for Your promises, Your protection, Your faithfulness, and Your love. Just as You have been faithful to me, Lord, let me be faithful to You, today and every day. Amen

15

GOD CANNOT FORSAKE CHRIST'S TEACHINGS

*Anyone who listens to my teaching and
obeys me is wise, like a person who builds
a house on solid rock. Though the rain comes in
torrents and the floodwaters rise and the winds
beat against that house, it won't collapse,
because it is built on rock.*

—

MATTHEW 7:24-25 NLT

THE BIG IDEA

God makes His wisdom available to you.
Your job is to acknowledge, to understand,
and (above all) to use that wisdom.

GOD'S WISDOM NEVER FAILS

God has made this promise to you: He will instruct you in the way you should go. God is always willing to teach, and you should always be willing to learn . . . but sometimes, you will be tempted to ignore God's instruction. Don't do it—instead of ignoring God, start praying about your situation . . . and start listening!

When we sincerely offer heartfelt prayers to our Heavenly Father, He will give direction and meaning to our lives—but He won't force us to follow Him. To the contrary, God has given us the free will to follow His commandments . . . or not. When we stray from God's

God will give direction and meaning to our lives.

commandments, we invite bitter consequences. But, when we follow His commandments—and when we genuinely and humbly seek His instruction—God touches our hearts and leads us on the path of His choosing.

Will you trust God to teach you "in the way you should go"? And will you make Christ's teachings the cornerstone of your life? Prayerfully, you will, because to do otherwise is not only the opposite of wisdom; it is also the prelude to disaster.

MORE FROM GOD'S WORD

The fear of the Lord is the beginning of wisdom; a good understanding have all those who do His commandments. His praise endures forever.

PSALM 111:10 NKJV

A wise man will hear and increase learning, and a man of understanding will attain wise counsel.

PROVERBS 1:5 NKJV

Teach me, O Lord, the way of Your statutes, and I shall keep it to the end.

PSALM 119:33 NKJV

So teach us to number our days, that we may gain a heart of wisdom.

PSALM 90:12 NKJV

Acquire wisdom—how much better it is than gold! And acquire understanding—it is preferable to silver.

PROVERBS 16:16 HCSB

MORE BIG IDEAS ABOUT WISDOM

Knowledge is horizontal. Wisdom is vertical; it comes down from above.

BILLY GRAHAM

God's plan for our guidance is for us to grow gradually in wisdom before we get to the cross roads.

BILL HYBELS

The more wisdom enters our hearts, the more we will be able to trust our hearts in difficult situations.

JOHN ELDREDGE

Wisdom is the God-given ability to see life with rare objectivity and to handle life with rare stability.

CHARLES SWINDOLL

Wisdom takes us beyond the realm of mere right and wrong. Wisdom takes into account our personalities, our strengths, our weaknesses, and even our present state of mind.

CHARLES STANLEY

Wise people listen to wise instruction, especially instruction from the Word of God.

WARREN WIERSBE

If you lack knowledge, go to school. If you lack wisdom, get on your knees.

VANCE HAVNER

The fruit of wisdom is Christlikeness, peace, humility, and love. And, the root of it is faith in Christ as the manifested wisdom of God.

J. I. PACKER

Patience is the companion of wisdom.

ST. AUGUSTINE

Most of us go through life praying a little, planning a little, jockeying for position, hoping but never being quite certain of anything, and always secretly afraid that we will miss the way. This is a tragic waste of truth and never gives rest to the heart. There is a better way. It is to repudiate our own wisdom and take instead the infinite wisdom of God.

A. W. TOZER

The man who prays
ceases to be a fool.

—

OSWALD CHAMBERS

THOUGHTS ABOUT WHAT GOD CAN DO

A PRAYER FOR TODAY

Dear Lord, when I trust in the wisdom of the world, I am often led astray, but when I trust in Your wisdom, I build my life upon a firm foundation. Today and every day I will trust Your Word and follow it, knowing that the ultimate wisdom is Your wisdom and the ultimate truth is Your truth. Amen

16

GOD CANNOT
TURN A DEAF EAR
TO YOUR PRAYERS

The LORD sees every heart and understands
and knows every plan and thought.
If you seek him, you will find him.

—

1 CHRONICLES 28:9 NLT

THE BIG IDEA

Prayer changes things—and you—so pray.

THE POWER OF PRAYER

"The power of prayer": these words are so familiar, yet sometimes we forget what they mean. Prayer is a powerful tool for communicating with our Creator; it is an opportunity to commune with the Giver of all things good. Prayer is not a thing to be taken lightly or to be used infrequently.

All too often, amid the rush of daily life, we may lose sight of God's presence in our lives. Instead of turning to Him for guidance and for comfort, we depend, instead, upon our own resources. To do so is a profound mistake. Prayer should never be reserved for mealtimes or for bedtimes; it should be an ever-present focus in our daily lives.

In his first letter to the Thessalonians, Paul wrote, "Rejoice evermore. Pray without ceasing. In every thing give thanks: for this is the will of God in Christ Jesus concerning you" (vv. 5:17-18 KJV). Paul's words apply to every Christian of every generation.

God cannot ignore your prayers; He hears them all. So

Prayer should be an ever-present focus in our daily lives.

today, instead of turning things over in your mind, turn them over to Him in prayer. Instead of worrying about your decisions, trust God to help you make them. Today, pray constantly about things great and small. God is listening, and He wants to hear from you. Now.

MORE FROM GOD'S WORD

The intense prayer of the righteous is very powerful.

JAMES 5:16 HCSB

Let the words of my mouth and the meditation of my heart be acceptable in Your sight, O Lord, my strength and my Redeemer.

PSALM 19:14 NKJV

Yet He often withdrew to deserted places and prayed.

LUKE 5:16 HCSB

Don't worry about anything, but in everything, through prayer and petition with thanksgiving, let your requests be made known to God.

PHILIPPIANS 4:6 HCSB

Rejoice in hope; be patient in affliction; be persistent in prayer.

ROMANS 12:12 HCSB

MORE BIG IDEAS ABOUT PRAYER

A life growing in its purity and devotion will be a more prayerful life.

E. M. BOUNDS

Find a place to pray where no one imagines that you are praying. Then, shut the door and talk to God.

OSWALD CHAMBERS

Prayer guards hearts and minds and causes God to bring peace out of chaos.

BETH MOORE

Two wings are necessary to lift our souls toward God: prayer and praise. Prayer asks. Praise accepts the answer.

MRS. CHARLES E. COWMAN

We forget that God sometimes has to say "No." We pray to Him as our heavenly Father, and like wise human fathers, He often says, "No," not from whim or caprice, but from wisdom, from love, and from knowing what is best for us.

PETER MARSHALL

When we pray, the first thing we should do is to see to it that we really get an audience with God, that we really get into His very presence. Before a word of petition is offered, we should have the definite consciousness that we are talking to God, and we should believe that He is listening.

R. A. TORREY

I learned as never before that persistent calling upon the Lord breaks through every stronghold of the devil, for nothing is impossible with God. For Christians in these troubled times, there is simply no other way.

JIM CYMBALA

What of the great prayer Jesus taught us to pray? It is for His kingdom and His will, yet we ought not to ask it unless we ourselves are prepared to cooperate.

ELISABETH ELLIOT

God knows that we, with our limited vision, don't even know that for which we should pray. When we entrust our requests to him, we trust him to honor our prayers with holy judgment.

MAX LUCADO

The real reason for a prayer is
intimacy with our Father.

—

OSWALD CHAMBERS

THOUGHTS ABOUT WHAT GOD CAN DO

A PRAYER FOR TODAY

Dear Lord, let me raise my hopes and my dreams, my worries and my fears to You. Let me be a worthy example to family and friends, showing them the importance and the power of prayer. Let me take everything to You in prayer, Lord, and when I do, let me trust in Your answers. Amen

17

GOD CANNOT STOP CARING ABOUT YOU

Humble yourselves therefore under the mighty
hand of God, so that He may exalt you
in due time, casting all your care upon Him,
because He cares about you.

—

1 PETER 5:6-7 HCSB

THE BIG IDEA

God will always comfort you so that you,
in turn, can have the strength
to comfort others.

HE HAS PROMISED TO COMFORT YOU

As Christians, we can be assured of this fact: Whether we find ourselves on the pinnacle of the mountain or in the darkest depths of the valley, God is there.

If you have been touched by the transforming love of Jesus, then you have every reason to live courageously. After all, Christ has already won the ultimate battle—and He won it for you—on the cross at Calvary. Still, even if you are a dedicated Christian, you may find yourself discouraged by the inevitable disappointments and tragedies that occur in the lives of believers and non-believers alike.

God is your protector and your deliverer.

The next time you find your courage tested to the limit, lean upon God's promises. Trust His Son. Remember that God is always near and that He is your protector and your deliverer. When you are worried, anxious, or afraid, call upon Him and accept the touch of His comforting hand. Remember that God rules both mountaintops and valleys—with limitless wisdom and love—now and forever.

MORE FROM GOD'S WORD

God has called us to peace.

1 CORINTHIANS 7:15 NKJV

Be of good comfort, be of one mind, live in peace; and the God of love and peace will be with you.

2 CORINTHIANS 13:11 NKJV

You will seek Me and find Me when you search for Me with all your heart.

JEREMIAH 29:13 HCSB

The Lord is near all who call out to Him, all who call out to Him with integrity. He fulfills the desires of those who fear Him; He hears their cry for help and saves them.

PSALM 145:18-19 HCSB

Surely goodness and mercy shall follow me all the days of my life: and I will dwell in the house of the Lord for ever.

PSALM 23:6 KJV

MORE BIG IDEAS ABOUT GOD'S COMFORT

Pour out your heart to God and tell Him how you feel. Be real, be honest, and when you get it all out, you'll start to feel the gradual covering of God's comforting presence.

BILL HYBELS

To know that God rules over all—that there are no accidents in life, that no tactic of Satan or man can ever thwart the will of God—brings divine comfort.

KAY ARTHUR

When I am criticized, injured, or afraid, there is a Father who is ready to comfort me.

MAX LUCADO

You don't have to be alone in your hurt! Comfort is yours. Joy is an option. And it's all been made possible by your Savior. He went without comfort so you might have it. He postponed joy so you might share in it. He willingly chose isolation so you might never be alone in your hurt and sorrow.

JONI EARECKSON TADA

Put your hand into the hand of God. He gives the calmness and serenity of heart and soul.

MRS. CHARLES E. COWMAN

We all go through pain and sorrow, but the presence of God, like a warm, comforting blanket, can shield us and protect us, and allow the deep inner joy to surface, even in the most devastating circumstances.

BARBARA JOHNSON

He is always thinking about us. We are before his eyes. The Lord's eye never sleeps, but is always watching out for our welfare. We are continually on his heart.

C. H. SPURGEON

He treats us as sons, and all he asks in return is that we shall treat Him as a Father whom we can trust without anxiety. We must take the son's place of dependence and trust, and we must let Him keep the father's place of care and responsibility.

HANNAH WHITALL SMITH

When God allows extraordinary
trials for His people,
He prepares extraordinary
comforts for them.

—

CORRIE TEN BOOM

THOUGHTS ABOUT WHAT GOD CAN DO

_____

_____

_____

_____

_____

_____

_____

_____

_____

_____

A PRAYER FOR TODAY

_Dear Lord, thank You for Your comfort. You lift me up when
I am disappointed. You protect me in times of trouble. Today,
I will be mindful of Your love, Your wisdom, and Your grace.
Amen_

18

GOD CANNOT
WITHHOLD HIS
BLESSINGS WHEN
YOU TRUST
HIS TIMING

Wait on the LORD, and he shall save thee.

—

PROVERBS 20:22 KJV

THE BIG IDEA

You don't know precisely what you need
—or when you need it—but God does.
So trust His timing.

TRUST HIS TIMING

Usually, we want God to provide us with easy answers to our questions and quick solutions to our problems. But oftentimes He has other plans. When we find ourselves waiting for God to respond to our prayers, we need both patience and wisdom: the patience to endure tough times and the wisdom to trust God's plans.

The Bible teaches us to trust God's timing in all matters, but we are sorely tempted to do otherwise. When we are beset with problems, we are understandably anxious for the tough times to reach a quick conclusion. We know that our suffering will end some day, and we want it to end NOW. God, however, works on His own timetable, and His schedule does not always coincide with ours.

God's plans are perfect; ours most certainly are not. So we must learn to trust the Father in good times and hard times. No exceptions.

Elisabeth Elliot advised, "We must learn to move according to the timetable of the Timeless One, and to be at peace." And Billy Graham observed, "As we wait on God, He helps us use the winds of adversity to soar above our problems."

So today, as you meet the challenges of everyday life, do your best to turn everything over to God. Whatever "it" is, He can handle it. And you can be sure that He will handle it when the time is right.

MORE FROM GOD'S WORD

Therefore the Lord is waiting to show you mercy, and is rising up to show you compassion, for the Lord is a just God. Happy are all who wait patiently for Him.

ISAIAH 30:18 HCSB

But those who wait on the LORD shall renew their strength; they shall mount up with wings like eagles, they shall run and not be weary, they shall walk and not faint.

ISAIAH 40:31 NKJV

To everything there is a season, a time for every purpose under heaven.

ECCLESIASTES 3:1 NKJV

I waited patiently for the LORD; and He inclined to me, and heard my cry.

PSALM 40:1 NKJV

Wait on the LORD; be of good courage, and He shall strengthen your heart; wait, I say, on the LORD!

PSALM 27:14 NKJV

MORE BIG IDEAS ABOUT GOD'S TIMING

God never hurries. There are no deadlines against which He must work. To know this is to quiet our spirits and relax our nerves.

A. W. TOZER

Will not the Lord's time be better than your time?

C. H. SPURGEON

God is in no hurry. Compared to the works of mankind, He is extremely deliberate. God is not a slave to the human clock.

CHARLES SWINDOLL

Waiting on God brings us to the journey's end quicker than our feet.

MRS. CHARLES E. COWMAN

God has a designated time when his promise will be fulfilled and the prayer will be answered.

JIM CYMBALA

When we read of the great Biblical leaders, we see that it was not uncommon for God to ask them to wait, not just a day or two, but for years, until God was ready for them to act.

GLORIA GAITHER

He whose attitude towards Christ is correct does indeed ask "in His Name" and receives what he asks for if it is something which does not stand in the way of his salvation. He gets it, however, only when he ought to receive it, for certain things are not refused us, but their granting is delayed to a fitting time.

ST. AUGUSTINE

By his wisdom, he orders his delays so that they prove to be far better than our hurries.

C. H. SPURGEON

We must leave it to God to answer our prayers in His own wisest way. Sometimes, we are so impatient and think that God does not answer. God always answers! He never fails! Be still. Abide in Him.

MRS. CHARLES E. COWMAN

God knows not only what we need
but also when we need it.
His timing is always perfect.

—

ELISABETH ELLIOT

THOUGHTS ABOUT WHAT GOD CAN DO

A PRAYER FOR TODAY

Dear Lord, Your wisdom is infinite, and the timing of Your Heavenly plan is perfect. You have a plan for my life that is grander than I can imagine. When I am impatient, remind me that You are never early or late. You are always on time, Father, so let me trust in You. Amen

19

GOD CANNOT
BE IMPERFECT
OR UNJUST

For I will proclaim the Lord's name.
Declare the greatness of our God!
The Rock—His work is perfect;
all His ways are entirely just. A faithful God,
without prejudice, He is righteous and true.

—

DEUTERONOMY 32:3-4 HCSB

THE BIG IDEA

God is good, and His truth endures forever.
Every new day provides opportunities
to praise Him, to love Him,
and to obey His Word.

HIS PLANS ARE PERFECT

Do you want to experience a life filled with abundance and peace? If so, here's a word of warning: you'll need to resist the temptation to do things "your way" and commit, instead, to do things God's way.

God has plans for your life. Big plans. Perfect plans. But He won't force you to follow His will; to the contrary, He has given you free will, the ability to make decisions on your own. With the freedom to choose comes the responsibility of living with the consequences of the choices you make.

The most important decision of your life is, of course, your commitment to accept Jesus Christ as your personal Lord and Savior. And once your eternal destiny is secured, you will undoubtedly ask yourself the question, "What now, Lord?" If you earnestly seek God's will for your life, you will find it . . . in time.

When you make the decision to seek God's will for your life, you will contemplate His Word, and you will be watchful for His signs. You will associate with fellow believers who will encourage your spiritual growth. You will listen to that inner voice that speaks to you in the quiet moments of your daily devotionals.

Sometimes, God's plans are crystal clear, but other times, He

God intends to use you in wonderful, unexpected ways.

leads you through the wilderness before He delivers you to the Promised Land. So be patient, keep searching, and keep praying. If you do, then in time, God will answer your prayers and make His plans known.

God is right here, and He intends to use you in wonderful, unexpected ways. You'll discover those plans by doing things His way . . . and you'll be eternally grateful that you did.

God is faithful, by whom you were called into the fellowship of His Son, Jesus Christ our Lord.

—

1 CORINTHIANS 1:9 NKJV

MORE FROM GOD'S WORD

I will sing of the tender mercies of the Lord forever! Young and old will hear of your faithfulness. Your unfailing love will last forever. Your faithfulness is as enduring as the heavens.

PSALM 89:1-2 NLT

Because of the LORD'S great love we are not consumed, for his compassions never fail. They are new every morning; great is your faithfulness.

LAMENTATIONS 3:22-23 NIV

For the Lord is good. His unfailing love continues forever, and his faithfulness continues to each generation.

PSALM 100:5 NLT

Blessed is he whose help is the God of Jacob, whose hope is in the LORD his God, the Maker of heaven and earth, the sea, and everything in them—the LORD, who remains faithful forever.

PSALM 146:5-6 NIV

MORE BIG IDEAS ABOUT GOD'S PROMISES

We honor God by asking for great things when they are a part of His promise. We dishonor Him and cheat ourselves when we ask for molehills where He has promised mountains.

VANCE HAVNER

God's promises are medicine for the broken heart. Let Him comfort you. And, after He has comforted you, try to share that comfort with somebody else. It will do both of you good.

WARREN WIERSBE

Never doubt in the dark what God told you in the light.

V. RAYMOND EDMAN

Faith is confidence in the promises of God or confidence that God will do what He has promised.

CHARLES STANLEY

The Rock of Ages is the great sheltering encirclement.

OSWALD CHAMBERS

The meaning of hope isn't just some flimsy wishing. It's a firm confidence in God's promises—that he will ultimately set things right.

SHEILA WALSH

We can have full confidence in God's promises because we can have full faith in His character.

FRANKLIN GRAHAM

In Biblical worship you do not find the repetition of a phrase; instead, you find the worshipers rehearsing the character of God and His ways, reminding Him of His faithfulness and His wonderful promises.

KAY ARTHUR

Gather the riches of God's promises which can strengthen you in the time when there will be no freedom.

CORRIE TEN BOOM

The stars may fall, but God's promises will stand and be fulfilled.

J. I. PACKER

God's promises are overflowings
from his great heart.

—

C. H. SPURGEON

THOUGHTS ABOUT WHAT GOD CAN DO

A PRAYER FOR TODAY

Lord, You have given me so much, and I am thankful. I know that every good thing You give me is to be shared with others. I give thanks for Your gifts . . . and I will share them. Amen

20

GOD CANNOT
DEPRIVE YOU OF
ETERNAL LIFE
IF YOU BELIEVE
IN HIS SON

For God so loved the world, that he gave his only begotten Son, that whosoever believeth in him should not perish, but have everlasting life.

—

JOHN 3:16 KJV

THE BIG IDEA

God offers you life abundant and life eternal.
If you have not accepted His gift,
the appropriate moment to do so is now.

THE PROMISE OF ETERNAL LIFE

Your life here on earth is merely a preparation for a far different life to come: the eternal life that God promises to those who welcome His Son into their hearts.

As a mere mortal, your vision for the future is finite. God's vision is not burdened by such limitations: His plans extend throughout all eternity. Thus, God's plans for you are not limited to the ups and downs of everyday life. Your Heavenly Father has bigger things in mind . . . much bigger things.

How marvelous it is that God became a man and walked among us. Had He not chosen to do so, we might feel removed from a distant Creator. But ours is not a distant God. Ours is a God who understands—far better than we ever could—the essence of what it means to be human.

God promises eternal life to those who welcome Jesus into their hearts.

God understands our hopes, our fears, and our temptations. He understands what it means to be angry and what it costs to forgive. He knows the heart, the conscience, and the soul of every person who has ever lived, including you.

As you struggle with the inevitable hardships and occasional disappointments of life, remember that God has invited you to accept His abundance not only for today but also for all eternity. So keep things in perspective. Although you will inevitably encounter occasional defeats in this world, you'll have all eternity to celebrate the ultimate victory in the next.

It is in giving that we receive,
it is in pardoning that we are pardoned,
it is in dying that we are born to eternal life.

—

ST. FRANCIS

MORE FROM GOD'S WORD

And this is the testimony: God has given us eternal life, and this life is in His Son. The one who has the Son has life. The one who doesn't have the Son of God does not have life.

1 JOHN 5:11-12 HCSB

We do not want you to be uninformed, brothers, concerning those who are asleep, so that you will not grieve like the rest, who have no hope. Since we believe that Jesus died and rose again, in the same way God will bring with Him those who have fallen asleep through Jesus.

1 THESSALONIANS 4:13-14 HCSB

Pursue righteousness, godliness, faith, love, endurance, and gentleness. Fight the good fight for the faith; take hold of eternal life, to which you were called and have made a good confession before many witnesses.

1 TIMOTHY 6:11-12 HCSB

I have written these things to you who believe in the name of the Son of God, so that you may know that you have eternal life.

1 JOHN 5:13 HCSB

MORE BIG IDEAS ABOUT ETERNAL LIFE

Teach us to set our hopes on heaven, to hold firmly to the promise of eternal life, so that we can withstand the struggles and storms of this world.

MAX LUCADO

Christ is the only liberator whose liberation lasts forever.

MALCOLM MUGGERIDGE

Your choice to either receive or reject the Lord Jesus Christ will determine where you spend eternity.

ANNE GRAHAM LOTZ

If you are a believer, your judgment will not determine your eternal destiny. Christ's finished work on Calvary was applied to you the moment you accepted Christ as Savior.

BETH MOORE

And because we know Christ is alive, we have hope for the present and hope for life beyond the grave.

BILLY GRAHAM

I can still hardly believe it. I, with shriveled, bent fingers, atrophied muscles, gnarled knees, and no feeling from the shoulders down, will one day have a new body—light, bright and clothed in righteousness—powerful and dazzling.

JONI EARECKSON TADA

God has promised us abundance, peace, and eternal life. These treasures are ours for the asking; all we must do is claim them. One of the great mysteries of life is why on earth do so many of us wait so very long to lay claim to God's gifts?

MARIE T. FREEMAN

The damage done to us on this earth will never find its way into that safe city. We can relax, we can rest, and though some of us can hardly imagine it, we can prepare to feel safe and secure for all of eternity.

BILL HYBELS

God did not spring forth from eternity; He brought forth eternity.

C. H. SPURGEON

Let us see the victorious Jesus,
the conqueror of the tomb,
the one who defied death.
And let us be reminded that
we, too, will be granted
the same victory.

—

MAX LUCADO

THOUGHTS ABOUT WHAT GOD CAN DO

A PRAYER FOR TODAY

Lord, I am only here on this earth for a brief while. But, You have offered me the priceless gift of eternal life through Your Son Jesus. I accept Your gift, Lord, with thanksgiving and praise. Let me share the good news of my salvation with those who need Your healing touch. Amen

APPENDIX

100 BIBLE VERSES YOU SHOULD KNOW

There are some Bible verses that are so important, so crucial to the Christian faith, that every believer should know them by heart. Can you focus on just 100 of these verses? Of course you can; of course you should.

The following pages contain 100 verses that you've probably heard many times before. These verses are short enough, and memorable enough, for you to place safely in your long-term mental database. So do yourself and your loved ones a favor: study each verse and do your best to place it permanently in your mind and in your heart. When you do, you'll discover that having God's Word in your heart is even better than having a Bible on your bookshelf.

VERSE 1

For God so loved the world, that he gave his only begotten Son, that whosoever believeth in him should not perish, but have everlasting life.

JOHN 3:16 KJV

VERSE 2

This is the day which the LORD hath made; we will rejoice and be glad in it.

PSALM 118:24 KJV

VERSE 3

In the beginning God created the heavens and the earth. The earth was without form, and void; and darkness was on the face of the deep. And the Spirit of God was hovering over the face of the waters. Then God said, "Let there be light"; and there was light.

GENESIS 1:1-3 NKJV

VERSE 4

After this manner therefore pray ye: Our Father which art
in heaven, Hallowed be thy name. Thy kingdom come.
Thy will be done in earth, as it is in heaven. Give us this day
our daily bread. And forgive us our debts, as we forgive our
debtors. And lead us not into temptation, but deliver us
from evil: For thine is the kingdom, and the power,
and the glory, for ever. Amen

MATTHEW 6:9-13 KJV

VERSE 5

The Lord is my shepherd; I shall not want.
He makes me to lie down in green pastures;
He leads me beside the still waters. He restores my soul.

PSALM 23:1-3 NKJV

VERSE 6

But grow in the grace and knowledge of our Lord and Savior
Jesus Christ. To Him be the glory both now and forever.

2 PETER 3:18 NKJV

VERSE 7

But those who wait on the Lord shall renew their strength;
they shall mount up with wings like eagles, they shall run
and not be weary, they shall walk and not faint.
ISAIAH 40:31 NKJV

VERSE 8

Be still, and know that I am God….
PSALM 46:10 KJV

VERSE 9

And now abide faith, hope, love, these three;
but the greatest of these is love.
1 CORINTHIANS 13:13 NKJV

VERSE 10

Trust in the Lord with all your heart, and lean not
on your own understanding; in all your ways
acknowledge Him, and He shall direct your paths.
PROVERBS 3:5-6 NKJV

VERSE 11

But seek first the kingdom of God and His righteousness, and all these things shall be added to you. Therefore do not worry about tomorrow, for tomorrow will worry about its own things. Sufficient for the day is its own trouble.

MATTHEW 6:33-34 NKJV

VERSE 12

I am the vine, you are the branches. He who abides in Me, and I in him, bears much fruit; for without Me you can do nothing.

JOHN 15:5 NKJV

VERSE 13

Ask, and it will be given to you; seek, and you will find; knock, and it will be opened to you. For everyone who asks receives, and he who seeks finds, and to him who knocks it will be opened.

MATTHEW 7:7-8 NKJV

VERSE 14

You shall have no other gods before Me.
EXODUS 20:3 NKJV

VERSE 15

I am come that they might have life,
and that they might have it more abundantly.
JOHN 10:10 KJV

VERSE 16

Choose for yourselves today the one you will worship . . . .
As for me and my family, we will worship the Lord.
JOSHUA 24:15 HCSB

VERSE 17

For by grace you are saved through faith,
and this is not from yourselves; it is God's gift—
not from works, so that no one can boast.
EPHESIANS 2:8-9 HCSB

VERSE 18

*Everyone must be quick to hear, slow to speak,
and slow to anger, for man's anger does not accomplish
God's righteousness.*
JAMES 1:19-20 HCSB

VERSE 19

*Therefore, whatever you want others to do for you,
do also the same for them—this is the Law and the Prophets.*
MATTHEW 7:12 HCSB

VERSE 20

*Cast thy burden upon the LORD, and he shall sustain thee:
he shall never suffer the righteous to be moved.*
PSALM 55:22 KJV

VERSE 21

*You will show me the path of life; in Your presence is fullness
of joy; at Your right hand are pleasures forevermore.*
PSALM 16:11 NKJV

VERSE 22

Now by this we know that we know Him,
if we keep His commandments.
1 JOHN 2:3 NKJV

VERSE 23

All Scripture is given by inspiration of God, and is profitable
for doctrine, for reproof, for correction, for instruction
in righteousness, that the man of God may be complete,
thoroughly equipped for every good work.
2 TIMOTHY 3:16-17 NKJV

VERSE 24

To everything there is a season,
a time for every purpose under heaven.
ECCLESIASTES 3:1 NKJV

VERSE 25

Guard your heart above all else, for it is the source of life.
PROVERBS 4:23 HCSB

VERSE 26

*Then He said to them all, "If anyone desires to come
after Me, let him deny himself, and take up his cross daily,
and follow Me. For whoever desires to save his life will lose it,
but whoever loses his life for My sake will save it."*
LUKE 9:23-24 NKJV

VERSE 27

*As the Father loved Me, I also have loved you;
abide in My love.*
JOHN 15:9 NKJV

VERSE 28

*These things have I spoken unto you, that my joy might
remain in you, and that your joy might be full.*
JOHN 15:11 KJV

VERSE 29

Rejoice in the Lord always. Again I will say, rejoice!
PHILIPPIANS 4:4 NKJV

VERSE 30

The greatest among you must be a servant.
But those who exalt themselves will be humbled,
and those who humble themselves will be exalted.

MATTHEW 23:11-12 NKJV

VERSE 31

Do not judge, and you will not be judged.
Do not condemn, and you will not be condemned.
Forgive, and you will be forgiven.

LUKE 6:37 HCSB

VERSE 32

Finally, brethren, whatever things are true, whatever things
are noble, whatever things are just, whatever things are pure,
whatever things are lovely, whatever things are of good report,
if there is any virtue and if there is anything praiseworthy—
meditate on these things.

PHILIPPIANS 4:8 NKJV

VERSE 33

*Assuredly, I say to you, inasmuch as you did it to one of the
least of these My brethren, you did it to Me.*
MATTHEW 25:40 NKJV

VERSE 34

*I have come as a light into the world,
that whoever believes in Me should not abide in darkness.*
JOHN 12:46 NKJV

VERSE 35

*Unless the Lord builds a house, its builders labor over it in
vain; unless the Lord watches over a city,
the watchman stays alert in vain.*
PSALM 127:1 HSCB

VERSE 36

Blessed are the merciful, because they will be shown mercy.
MATTHEW 5:7 HCSB

VERSE 37

Make no friendship with an angry man,
and with a furious man do not go,
lest you learn his ways and set a snare for your soul.
PROVERBS 22:24-25 NKJV

VERSE 38

But Jesus looked at them and said to them,
"With men this is impossible,
but with God all things are possible."
MATTHEW 19:26 NKJV

VERSE 39

Make a joyful noise unto the LORD, all ye lands.
Serve the LORD with gladness:
come before his presence with singing.
PSALM 100:1-2 KJV

VERSE 40

God is our refuge and strength, a very present help in trouble.
PSALM 46:1 NKJV

VERSE 41

Weeping may endure for a night,
but joy comes in the morning.
PSALM 30:5 NKJV

VERSE 42

Jesus said to him, "'You shall love the Lord your God with
all your heart, with all your soul, and with all your mind.'
This is the first and great commandment."
MATTHEW 22:37-38 NKJV

VERSE 43

Blessed is the man who walks not in the counsel of
the ungodly, nor stands in the path of sinners,
nor sits in the seat of the scornful;
but his delight is in the law of the Lord,
and in His law he meditates day and night.
PSALM 1:1-2 NKJV

VERSE 44

Be strong and courageous, and do the work.
Do not be afraid or discouraged, for the Lord God,
my God, is with you.
1 CHRONICLES 28:20 NIV

VERSE 45

The LORD is gracious and full of compassion,
slow to anger and great in mercy. The LORD is good to all,
and His tender mercies are over all His works.
PSALM 145:8-9 NKJV

VERSE 46

Love is patient; love is kind. Love does not envy;
is not boastful; is not conceited; does not act improperly;
is not selfish; is not provoked; does not keep a record
of wrongs; finds no joy in unrighteousness,
but rejoices in the truth; bears all things, believes all things,
hopes all things, endures all things.
1 CORINTHIANS 13:4-7 HCSB

VERSE 47

Beloved, if God so loved us,
we also ought to love one another.
1 JOHN 4:11 NKJV

VERSE 48

Heaven and earth will pass away,
but My words will never pass away.
MATTHEW 24:35 HCSB

VERSE 49

Even though I walk through the valley of the shadow of death,
I will fear no evil, for you are with me;
your rod and your staff, they comfort me.
PSALM 23:4 NIV

VERSE 50

Therefore, whether you eat or drink, or whatever you do,
do all to the glory of God.
1 CORINTHIANS 10:31 NKJV

VERSE 51

No one can be a slave of two masters, since either he
will hate one and love the other, or be devoted to one and
despise the other. You cannot be slaves of God and of money.
MATTHEW 6:24 HCSB

VERSE 52

If you have faith as a mustard seed,
you will say to this mountain, "Move from here to there,"
and it will move; and nothing will be impossible for you.
MATTHEW 17:20 NKJV

VERSE 53

Go, therefore, and make disciples of all nations,
baptizing them in the name of the Father and of the Son and
of the Holy Spirit, teaching them to observe everything
I have commanded you. And remember,
I am with you always, to the end of the age.
MATTHEW 28:19-20 HCSB

VERSE 54

Man does not see what the Lord sees,
for man sees what is visible, but the Lord sees the heart.
1 SAMUEL 16:7 HCSB

VERSE 55

Whoever conceals an offense promotes love,
but whoever gossips about it separates friends.
PROVERBS 17:9 HCSB

VERSE 56

I have set before you life and death, blessing and curse.
Choose life so that you and your descendants may live,
love the Lord your God, obey Him, and remain faithful to
Him. For He is your life, and He will prolong
your life in the land the Lord swore to give to your fathers
Abraham, Isaac, and Jacob.
DEUTERONOMY 30:19-20 HCSB

VERSE 57

The sensible see danger and take cover;
the foolish keep going and are punished.
PROVERBS 27:12 HCSB

VERSE 58

Be sober! Be on the alert!
Your adversary the Devil is prowling around
like a roaring lion, looking for anyone he can devour.
1 PETER 5:8 HCSB

VERSE 59

Rejoice always, pray without ceasing, in everything give
thanks; for this is the will of God in Christ Jesus for you.
1 THESSALONIANS 5:16-18 NKJV

VERSE 60

Be an example to the believers in word, in conduct,
in love, in spirit, in faith, in purity.
1 TIMOTHY 4:12 NKJV

VERSE 61

Now godliness with contentment is great gain.
For we brought nothing into this world,
and it is certain we can carry nothing out.
And having food and clothing, with these we shall be content.
1 TIMOTHY 6:6-8 NKJV

VERSE 62

Draw near to God, and He will draw near to you.
JAMES 4:8 HCSB

VERSE 63

The borrower is servant to the lender.
PROVERBS 22:7 NIV

VERSE 64

He did it with all his heart. So he prospered.
2 CHRONICLES 31:21 NKJV

VERSE 65

In fact, when we were with you,
this is what we commanded you:
"If anyone isn't willing to work, he should not eat."
2 THESSALONIANS 3:10 HCSB

VERSE 66

Therefore, if anyone is in Christ, he is a new creation;
old things have passed away;
behold, all things have become new.
2 CORINTHIANS 5:17 NKJV

VERSE 67

No temptation has overtaken you except such as
is common to man; but God is faithful, who will not
allow you to be tempted beyond what you are able,
but with the temptation will also make the way of escape,
that you may be able to bear it.
1 CORINTHIANS 10:13 NKJV

VERSE 68

Give thanks to the Lord, for He is good;
His faithful love endures forever.
PSALM 106:1 HCSB

VERSE 69

But this I say: He who sows sparingly will also reap sparingly,
and he who sows bountifully will also reap bountifully.
So let each one give as he purposes in his heart,
not grudgingly or of necessity; for God loves a cheerful giver.
2 CORINTHIANS 9:6-7 NKJV

VERSE 70

Should we accept only good from God and not adversity?
JOB 2:10 HCSB

VERSE 71

But be doers of the word,
and not hearers only, deceiving yourselves.
JAMES 1:22 NKJV

VERSE 72

So then, they are no longer two but one flesh.
Therefore what God has joined together, let not man separate.
MATTHEW 19:6 NKJV

VERSE 73

Blessed are those who hunger and thirst for righteousness,
because they will be filled.
MATTHEW 5:6 HCSB

VERSE 74

Therefore humble yourselves under the mighty hand of God,
that He may exalt you in due time,
casting all your care upon Him, for He cares for you.
1 PETER 5:6-7 NKJV

VERSE 75

In the same way faith, if it doesn't have works,
is dead by itself.
JAMES 2:17 HCSB

VERSE 76

So teach us to number our days,
that we may gain a heart of wisdom.
PSALM 90:12 NKJV

VERSE 77

Acquire wisdom—how much better it is than gold!
And acquire understanding—it is preferable to silver.
PROVERBS 16:16 HCSB

VERSE 78

But the fruit of the Spirit is love, joy, peace, patience,
kindness, goodness, faith, gentleness, self-control.
Against such things there is no law.
GALATIANS 5:22-23 HCSB

VERSE 79

Train up a child in the way he should go,
and when he is old he will not depart from it.
PROVERBS 22:6 NKJV

VERSE 80

When I was a child, I spoke as a child,
I understood as a child, I thought as a child;
but when I became a man, I put away childish things.
1 CORINTHIANS 13:11 NKJV

VERSE 81

Shepherd God's flock among you, not overseeing out of
compulsion but freely, according to God's will;
not for the money but eagerly.
1 PETER 5:2 HCSB

VERSE 82

All bitterness, anger and wrath, insult and slander must be
removed from you, along with all wickedness.
And be kind and compassionate to one another,
forgiving one another, just as God also forgave you in Christ.
EPHESIANS 4:31-32 HCSB

VERSE 83

Do not fear, for I am with you; do not be afraid,
for I am your God. I will strengthen you; I will help you;
I will hold on to you with My righteous right hand.
ISAIAH 41:10 HCSB

VERSE 84

The one who lives with integrity lives securely,
but whoever perverts his ways will be found out.
PROVERBS 10:9 HCSB

VERSE 85

On the first day of the week, very early in the morning,
they came to the tomb, bringing the spices they had prepared.
They found the stone rolled away from the tomb.
They went in but did not find the body of the Lord Jesus.
While they were perplexed about this, suddenly two men stood
by them in dazzling clothes. So the women were terrified and
bowed down to the ground. "Why are you looking for the
living among the dead?" asked the men.
"He is not here, but He has been resurrected!"
LUKE 24:1-6 HCSB

VERSE 86

*One thing I do, forgetting those things which are behind and
reaching forward to those things which are ahead,
I press toward the goal for the prize of the upward call
of God in Christ Jesus.*
PHILIPPIANS 3:13-14 NKJV

VERSE 87

*Therefore, get your minds ready for action,
being self-disciplined, and set your hope completely on
the grace to be brought to you at the revelation of Jesus Christ.*
1 PETER 1:13 HCSB

VERSE 88

A word fitly spoken is like apples of gold in settings of silver.
PROVERBS 25:11 NKJV

VERSE 89

Do not be deceived: "Bad company corrupts good morals."
1 CORINTHIANS 15:33 HCSB

VERSE 90

The one who conceals his sins will not prosper,
but whoever confesses and renounces them will find mercy.
PROVERBS 28:13 HCSB

VERSE 91

Commit your activities to the Lord
and your plans will be achieved.
PROVERBS 16:3 HCSB

VERSE 92

But when the Helper comes,
whom I shall send to you from the Father, the Spirit of truth
who proceeds from the Father, He will testify of Me.
JOHN 15:26 NKJV

VERSE 93

Pride goes before destruction,
and a haughty spirit before a fall.
PROVERBS 16:18 NKJV

VERSE 94

So he who had received five talents came and brought five
other talents, saying, "Lord, you delivered to me five talents;
look, I have gained five more talents besides them."
His lord said to him, "Well done, good and faithful servant;
you were faithful over a few things, I will make you ruler
over many things. Enter into the joy of your lord."
MATTHEW 25:20-21 NKJV

VERSE 95

If we confess our sins,
He is faithful and righteous to forgive us our sins
and to cleanse us from all unrighteousness.
1 JOHN 1:9 HCSB

VERSE 96

And you shall know the truth,
and the truth shall make you free.
JOHN 8:32 NKJV

VERSE 97

*Do not love the world or the things in the world.
If anyone loves the world, the love of the Father is not in him.*
1 JOHN 2:15 NKJV

VERSE 98

For I am the Lord, I do not change.
MALACHI 3:6 NKJV

VERSE 99

*You are the light of the world. A city that is set on a hill
cannot be hidden. Nor do they light a lamp and put it under a
basket, but on a lampstand, and it gives light to all who are in
the house. Let your light so shine before men, that they may
see your good works and glorify your Father in heaven.*
MATTHEW 5:14-16 NKJV

VERSE 100

*I was glad when they said unto me,
Let us go into the house of the LORD.*
PSALM 122:1 KJV

ABOUT THE AUTHOR

Dr. Criswell Freeman lives and writes in Nashville, Tennessee. He graduated from Vanderbilt University and from the Adler School of Professional Psychology in Chicago, where he earned his doctorate. He is a cofounder of Freeman-Smith, a division of Worthy Publishing. With hundreds of inspirational and devotional titles to his credit, and with over 20 million books in print, Dr. Freeman is a "quiet best-seller" in the Christian marketplace.